My
Leprechaun
Friends

My Leprechaun Friends

⁓⁓⁓

A TRUE STORY

⁓⁓⁓

LUCYLE DUBÉ

iUniverse, Inc.
Bloomington

My Leprechaun Friends
A True Story

iUniverse books may be ordered through booksellers or by contacting:

iUniverse
1663 Liberty Drive
Bloomington, IN 47403
www.iuniverse.com
1-800-Authors (1-800-288-4677)

ISBN: 978-1-4759-6636-7 (sc)
ISBN: 978-1-4759-6637-4 (ebk)

Library of Congress Control Number: 2013900053

Printed in the United States of America

iUniverse rev. date: 1/08/2013

Contents

Acknowledgments

Many special thanks to my dear friend Louise Delisle for her help with typing and editing the manuscript, and to Toraya Ayres who corrected the English language. Many thanks also to Barbara Brunner with whom I stayed for four months in Sedona, Arizona, and who suggested that I write my story in English.

Special thanks to Louise Gaudet, another friend of mine, who encouraged me to publish my story.

Introduction

I dedicate my book to everybody who believes in or who would like to believe that we live in a world full of magic and fantastic beings such as fairies, gnomes, and dragons.

Because we are unable to see them or feel them, we have difficulty believing that they could exist unless they decide to manifest themselves to us.

I have always been receptive to the possibility that different creatures or animals were living in other dimensions. As a child growing up, even if I could not see them, I knew deep inside that they were real and *real* they were because I *believed*.

It was during my stay at Barbara's house in Arizona, which was surrounded by roadrunners, that I decided to share my story. Everything in this book is true; only the names of the persons involved have been changed.

What made this experience possible was the fusion of my Irish heritage, the house I was living in, and my openness to accept that beings from another dimension could exist. Believe me! The visit of three leprechauns in my house—Gallaghan, Milady, and Woody, whom I call my Little People—was a real adventure. They lived with me for about fifteen years. They still occasionally visit to make sure I am well and that I still believe in magic.

Where did they come from? What were they doing in my house? Why were they living with my mother and me?

If you read my story, you will have all the answers to these questions.

One thing is certain. Since the visit of these Little People, my life has been full of magic and happiness.

Chapter 1

MY IRISH HERITAGE

I have Irish blood from my father's side of the family and American Indian Sioux blood from my mother's side. My father's mother was a typical, sweet Irish woman. She was small, had light reddish hair, and skin full of freckles. She was known as a *fey*, which means a magical person who knows many *things*, many of them invisible to our eyes.

My grandmother could talk with animals, birds, bees, and plants. She could understand them, and she had a very special relationship with them. Her garden was the most beautiful one around. People used to stop in front of her house to look at and buy vegetables, fruits, honey, and flowers. Some of them were a little envious to see her abundance of fruit trees, her flourishing garden, the beehives full of sweet honey, and all the animals attracted to her farm. The bees never stung her. She would thank them for their honey, talk with them, and appreciate how nice they were to her.

My mother's mother was a midwife, and she helped lots of people. She was also clairvoyant. She would always know who just passed away in the village.

My grandfather was always in the company of Indian people and learning their way of living and their way of surviving in these times of recession.

Chapter 2

LET THE MAGIC BEGIN!

My magical adventures with the leprechauns began many years ago, during a time when my mother and I moved from the city of Montreal, Quebec, to Ontario, Canada.

The house we moved into was big, two stories high, and located at the edge of a village. The rooms were so spacious you could roller skate in them, and there were many places for children to hide. We enjoyed the large house and appreciated that the previous owner had put in new rugs and painted every room.

Across the street from our house was a field of ornamental grass covered with birch and pine trees where a calm and clear river flowed through. In the back, beyond a mini-golf course, stood wonderful tall trees that reflected in the crystal water of a brook that wound around rocks and wildflowers on its way to the river. All the vegetation was so beautiful and smelled so lovely.

Some people from the village told me that many years ago, around the middle of the eighteenth century, our house was once the location of a very famous pub, the only one around for miles and favored by Irish farmers. Where the garage is now was once a stable for their horses. The pub was a meeting place for these immigrant people where every week they would share letters and news from their native land, have a good time, laugh, and sing.

On one beautiful spring morning as I walked along the brook's edge, I saw a huge rock near a very big tree. I decided to sit on that rock for a while to rest and enjoy the scenery. I noticed a fallen tree across the brook that made a natural bridge.

It was such a peaceful scene that with my eyes wide open, I started to dream. I wanted to be able to see some beings from other dimensions like elves and fairies that were also part of the nature kingdom even if I could not see them. I could almost feel their presence.

After half an hour dreaming about them, I decided to return home, thinking perhaps I would see them at another time, and when they got used to seeing me, they would learn to trust me. They would know that I would not harm them and that I would be willing to help them if they ever needed me. All my life, as long as I can remember, I always believed that one day I would be able to encounter them.

I returned home after my walk and sat down for breakfast. Something caught my attention. I saw something gleaming beside my left foot on the floor, and I bent my head down to have a better look. Intrigued, I stretched my arm to pick up the shining objects. My fingertips started to tingle, and a wave of energy rushed up my arm when I touched them. There were three silver hairpins lying underneath my shedding dog's hair. What a surprise! Where did they come from all of a sudden?

I did remember that the day before, on my shopping trip, I had bought some silver hairpins, and I put the package on a small table in one of the front rooms. Curious, I decided to go into that room to check it out, but first, I had to take the hook from the small door that allowed entrance to the front of the house. We kept that door locked during the night because Sam, my German shepherd, was not allowed in those rooms.

The room, where I left the pins the day before, was about thirty feet away from the kitchen table through the locked door. On the table lay the hairpin card. It held sixty pins in bunches of ten. I had not removed any of the new hairpins from the card, but I noticed in the first group that some of the pins were missing, and in the second group, some pins were loose. I tried to place the three hairpins that I had found on the floor in the kitchen back in the package. I even tried to make them tight like the rest, but it did not work. They remained loose.

"Well, well," I thought. "Something is strange!"

I didn't remove those hairpins and neither did my mother. The previous night she had gone to bed before me, and she was still sleeping. Nobody else lived with us in this house.

I went back into the kitchen to prepare some herb tea for my friend Johnny who was coming to see me around nine thirty. He barely had time to sit down before I said, "I'm almost sure we have a creature from another dimension living with us in the house."

"You sure do," he said. "And he is here now."

"Do you see him?" I asked.

"Yes, and he is a leprechaun."

By that time, Johnny was laughing. "He's right in front of you!"

"Where in front of me?"

"Leaning against the refrigerator. I can't believe you can't see him!"

"Can you ask his name?" I asked Johnny.

The Little One told Johnny, "My name is Gallaghan."

Johnny sees all kinds of creatures from other dimensions such as gnomes, elves, leprechauns, and fairies. I think he is very lucky because very few adults can see them. Children under five years old can see them and sometimes talk and play with them because adults have not tampered with their minds yet. Animals can see, talk, and play with them too.

I could not see or hear him, but I was happy to know that I had a little friend named Gallaghan visiting us from another dimension. He must have heard my call earlier when I was daydreaming near the brook. He must have decided it was time for me to see him. Such a privilege!

But I was not surprised to learn that a leprechaun was visiting us considering that our house used to be a gathering place for Irish farmers. As you probably know, leprechauns originated from Ireland, and they can live long lives—hundreds of years.

Gallaghan must have followed one of the Irish families, and after the family members died, he was left to roam and wait for somebody of Irish descent who, of course, believed in leprechauns.

But before we continue, I would like to take a few moments to talk about my friend Johnny.

Johnny used to come to my shop for a haircut. This was how I met him. He knew that I was helping people with their health and other problems. For a long time, he thought he was a very bad person because he had very strong powers and didn't know how to use them properly. So I gave him some quartz and taught him how to protect himself and how to use his power to help people.

He is one of the rare people whom I have met who is so powerful yet so timid about his power. To me, he was like a son, and when I needed help, he was always there. Now I needed Johnny's help to get answers to my questions about Gallaghan.

Chapter 3

PLEASE PAY ATTENTION!

A few weeks later, after that first encounter with Gallaghan, I realized I was not at the end of my surprises.

One day, my friend Sylvia and I were returning home from a flea market with bags of vegetables and fruits. Sylvia is about five feet eight inches tall, is strong, and stands very straight.

I used to tell her, "When you were young, you certainly swallowed a broomstick."

She would laugh and say many people told her that.

When there were only two bags left to carry inside, I said to her, "You sit and rest. I will bring the last bags in, and then I'll make you a cup of tea."

"Okay," she said.

We were both tired, but Sylvia appeared to be more tired than I was. She is six years older and always insists on carrying in the heaviest bag, like fifty pounds of dog food.

Sighing, I went to pick up the remaining two bags and brought them into the pantry. Suddenly, I felt a hand pushing me gently but firmly on my right buttock. Startled, I turned and asked Sylvia, who was sitting nearby, "Do you want something?"

I had already said I would make her some tea. What more did she want? At that moment, I wanted to sit down too.

"No," she said. "Why are you asking me?"

She was getting a little upset. She did not understand why I was asking that question.

"Why did you push me just then?"

"I never touched you."

"Don't get mad," I said. "It must have been the dog."

"You're dreaming," she said. "Look, the dog is sleeping over there in the solarium."

"Then it must have been Gallaghan," I told her.

"Who is Gallaghan?"

"He is our little friend, a leprechaun from another dimension."

She appeared stupefied, flabbergasted, and incredulous.

"Are you pulling my leg?" she asked.

"No!"

The way she looked at me—oh, la-la. She raised her eyebrows, her eyes narrowed, and her mouth became tight. She made a noise like, "Humph."

I could tell she thought I was lying or I was a nut or a crank. Smiling at her, I said, "Never mind. I can tell that you do not believe in these things."

I started to talk about other things, and that was the end of this matter for the day.

Sylvia lived on the second floor of an apartment complex across the street from my house. She used to watch everything that was going on in my house. She even bought some spyglasses to be able to see better through my two big front windows. Maybe it was just a bad habit of hers due to loneliness, or a kind of stress caused by her work, being in charge of two hundred girls at a factory in town. But she was a good woman, and she had a good heart. She used to cross the street to see if my mother and I needed help shopping.

Chapter 4

DO YOU BELIEVE NOW?

Following that event, some people had told me that Sylvia thought I was somewhat nutty.

"It doesn't matter what she thinks of me," I replied. "Someday she will get proof that Little People exist."

So do you know what I did? Let me tell you. Sometimes I like to confront people.

Sylvia used to come to our house three or four times a week, at night mostly, to play a tile game we called rummy. Perhaps you know this game. We would place the numbered tiles on a little stand and begin to play. Sylvia really enjoyed playing rummy with us.

My mother and I knew that sometimes Gallaghan liked to play tricks on our visitors. So, one night, I tried to contact him and ask him to do something that would make Sylvia believe in his existence; however, I did specify to him not to scare her too much.

One hour before she was due to arrive, my mother and I were chuckling aloud thinking about what I asked Gallaghan to do during the game.

When Sylvia arrived, my mother and I did not say a word about what we had planned.

After playing rummy for about half an hour, Sylvia's tile tray suddenly spilled on the table, tossing all her numbers around. My mother and I looked at each other and smiled, but we did not mention our plan. We knew that something else would happen, and when it did, it would be even stranger.

"What happened?" I asked Sylvia, pretending I didn't know.

"I don't know," she said, looking puzzled. "I wasn't touching it."

She picked up her tiles and placed them on her stand again.

Well, do you know, after playing another thirty-five minutes or so, Sylvia's whole tray flew in the air. The tray had been full of tiles. Some scattered on the table, but most of them fell all over the floor and some under the buffet.

I got up and helped her pick up the tiles from the table and the floor. As she was putting them back on her tray, I asked her again, "What happened? How did you do that?"

I was delighted with Gallaghan's trick.

"I don't know," said Sylvia. "I was not even touching the table, and my hands were on my lap. I really do not understand how the whole thing flew all over the place like that."

You should have seen the expression on her face. It was like a big question mark. She was looking at her tray like it was a wriggling snake.

My mother and I were laughing so much that by then I confessed to Sylvia.

"I asked Gallaghan to come and play a small trick, but not to scare you too much, so that you would at least believe that other Little People exist even if you cannot see them."

She did not reply to me. She turned around in her chair and, shaking a finger in the air, said, "Gallaghan, leave me alone. Do not do this to me anymore! I don't like it."

"Yes," I said. "He will leave you alone. He is a nice little man."

Gallaghan never did play one of his tricks on her again, and we never heard her talking about the impossibility of Little People living in our dimension. She knew then that sometimes they can visit humans and that they do not look exactly like us, but they are *real*. Now she *believed*.

But Sylvia was not the only one who had doubt. Another friend of mine, J. J., did too.

I meet J. J. in Montreal during an esoteric show held at the Place Bonaventure. People gathered and shared their knowledge about everything concerning New Age: conferences, music, crystals, books, and workshops. J. J. was a participant as a palm reader and an astrologer.

Curious, I asked him to read my palm. When he took my hand, a few tears rolled down my cheeks and he asked, "What's wrong?"

"I feel a very deep sorrow inside you," I told him.

"I am not surprised," he answered. "I can see in your hand that you are a healer."

Then I knew he was not a quack. I had confidence in him. I invited him to our house for a couple of days to read palms and draw astrological charts for my customers.

"Yes," he said, "I would be happy to be known again. I am just getting back to work, and I need to make some money."

A few weeks after my invitation, on a late afternoon, J. J. arrived at our house. I introduced him to my mother, and we all sat down for dinner. Then my mother started talking about the leprechaun, Gallaghan, and all the tricks he was playing on us and on a few of my customers.

"You can expect Gallaghan to play some tricks on you while you are staying here," my mother told him.

He asked a few questions, but we could tell he was skeptical. I knew deep down in my heart that he was uncomfortable with the subject about beings living in other dimensions.

We spent a pleasant evening together.

As I was taking him to the guest room, I told him, "Do not ask Gallaghan if he is real because he will have a big surprise for you. Also, tomorrow when you wake up, don't try to roll up the window shade because it is stuck. In the meantime, have a nice sleep and sweet dreams."

The last night J. J. was at our home, we all went to sleep around eleven o'clock. A few minutes after closing my bedroom door, as I was falling asleep, I heard the guest doorknob turning. "Oh! Oh!" I thought. "Somebody is visiting my friend."

A few minutes went by very quietly, and then I heard a big noise. The shade of the window in the guest room rolled up, and then everything was quiet again.

I kept listening to see what my friend would do. A minute or so later, I heard my friend get up from the bed, pull the shade to the middle of the window where it usually was stuck, and then he went back to bed.

The next morning, I asked him, "What happened?"

"I don't know," he said. "That shade suddenly zipped all the way up."

Then I told him what I had heard the night before.

My friend asked me, "Was it Gallaghan?"

"Yes," I said, "because that shade is really stuck. It goes down but never up. If you pull the shade down, I have to take it off the window, roll it up by hand, and put it back on the window. People who usually sleep in that room leave the shade where it is."

When my friend was leaving, he said, "I was not sure it was Gallaghan last night, but now I am."

He knew, like everybody who slept in that room, that the shade did not go up.

Later, I went upstairs to change the sheets and make the bed. I was curious about the window shade. I drew the shade down a little bit. Next, I pulled it to see if it would go up. It did. Three times, it went all the way up, and then it stopped in the middle of the window. It would not go up again. When I pulled it down half an inch, it would not go up, just the way it was before my guest had arrived.

Chapter 5

WHO TURNED ON THE LIGHT?

One morning my mother came down the stairs chuckling. "You will never guess what happened to me in the middle of the night."

"No," I said. "I did not hear anything. What happened?"

As she was sitting on her bed to put on her slippers, preparing to go to the bathroom, the small table lamp near the door of her bedroom turned on. She was taken aback for a few seconds, and then the surprise was gone. She knew who had done this.

"Thank you, Gallaghan," she said.

When she returned from the bathroom, she went directly to her bed without turning off the light. After settling in her bed, she said to Gallaghan, "You can turn the light off now. I do not need it anymore."

But nothing happened. After a few minutes, she had to get up and turn the light off herself.

"Why didn't he turn the light off?" asked Mother. "If he can turn the light on, he should be able to turn it off when I do not need it anymore."

"Don't ask too much of him," I said. "You know he likes to play. Probably he just went to sleep after turning on the light for you."

Shaking her head a little and laughing, she sat down to have breakfast.

It was her first direct experience with the Little People but not her last.

Chapter 6

A GLIMPSE AT GALLAGHAN

Early one rainy Sunday afternoon, the house was very quiet for a change. The telephone was not ringing, and we had no visitors. My mother decided to have a nap, so she went upstairs to her bedroom. After I finished the work I was doing, I also decided to take a nap. I did not go to my bedroom. Instead, I lay down on the futon downstairs and fell asleep. About an hour later, as I was waking up, my mother was coming down the stairs. Halfway down and talking very loudly, she asked, "Were you upstairs a few minutes ago? You just woke me up really well."

"Don't you see that I am still lying on the futon, and I'm half-asleep?" I replied.

"Excuse me," she said apologetically. "I really thought you were upstairs."

"Why did you think that?"

"Well," she said, "I heard somebody walking very fast, almost running. I rushed out of my bedroom, and near the stairs, I saw the whole profile of Gallaghan. He was starting to go downstairs. You should see the way he was dressed! His clothes were very colorful, red and green. He had on a very funny hat and pointy shoes. That's all I could see. He disappeared very fast from view."

After that, she said she turned and went into her room to pick up her shoes from the place she always put them. No shoes. Looking around, she said to herself, "Where are they? I never enter the room with my shoes on. I just leave them beside the door." And there they were, near her bed, beside each other in a perfect row, and placed exactly where she put her feet when she got out of bed. She knew then who did that.

"That is why I asked you. I wanted to be certain you did not go upstairs."

She was thrilled that Gallaghan had played one of his little tricks on her, and she was even more delighted to have been able to see him.

"Have you ever seen him?" she asked.

"No."

Then I told her she was very lucky because it is a privilege when leprechauns show themselves.

"Yes," she said with a big smile. "I am lucky."

Chapter 7

CHILDREN CAN SEE THEM TOO!

Remember, I was telling you that little children can see leprechauns. One of my sons and his family came to visit us for a weekend. He and his wife have two children, Jonathan and Benjamin. At that time, Jonathan was about two and half years old, and his brother, Benjamin, was about one and half years old. They were playing in the kitchen and having a lot of fun together.

Jonathan started to run. He was heading toward the front of the house where he was not supposed to go. I darted to catch him and bring him back to the kitchen, and then the funniest thing happened. Suddenly he stopped, looked in front of him, and started to laugh a good, hearty laugh. His back was still facing me. He was probably seeing Gallaghan.

After about five seconds, Jonathan raced again toward the front room. He was still laughing. Finally, I captured him and took him in my arms. He was still very happy. His eyes were dancing, and he was looking everywhere, trying to see Gallaghan. He could not tell me what he saw because he did not speak very well yet.

Later that afternoon, Benjamin was in my arms facing the table where everybody was sitting, but he kept turning his face toward the window at the back of my chair. I tried many times to turn him around, but he kept turning his head to look, probably at Gallaghan who was at the back of my chair. I am sure that when he stopped looking, it was because Gallaghan was gone.

Chapter 8

GALLAGHAN HAS A WIFE!

Now it is time to introduce you to Milady. Who is Milady? She is Gallaghan's wife. How did I find out she was his wife?

Well, it happened on a weekend when we had a guest.

A friend of mine, Cathy from Montreal, came to visit us for three days. She was not feeling very well. Because I am a healer, she knew that I could help her with her health issues, so I gave her some treatments, and we took it easy. Later we had dinner, and we start talking about Gallaghan.

"Are you sure?" she asked. "Is it really true? It is difficult to believe."

She was shaking her head and making a funny face. To us, her reaction was hilarious because everybody who hears about Gallaghan for the first time always makes funny faces. We spent a pleasant evening talking about other things, and then we went to bed around 11:00 p.m.

I had a good sleep.

During the night, about four inches of snow fell. When I got up, everything outside was covered with a white blanket: trees, streets, houses, and cars. After eating breakfast, I went outside to shovel the snow from the front door. Cathy was still sleeping.

Around ten o'clock, I was almost finished shoveling the snow. The front door opened. Cathy was standing there shivering and acting all excited.

"Guess what happened to me during the night!" she exclaimed.

"Go back in the house," I told her. "It's very cold out here. You will get sick standing there wearing only your pajamas. I'll come inside in a few minutes."

Five to ten minutes later, I went into the house saying to myself that Gallaghan must have visited her during the night, but there was a surprise for me also.

Cathy was still very excited. She was almost hopping up and down.

"Please," I begged her, "sit and tell me what happened to you."

"I was scared most of the night," she said. "I put all of the blankets over my head. There was so much noise in the bedroom I nearly called you, but I decided not to disturb you. I didn't have the courage to stick my head out of the blankets. Didn't you hear anything?"

"I didn't hear anything, and you should have called me because the leprechaun does not want to disturb me. If you would have told me, everything would have stopped."

"Leprechaun! You were telling the truth about your little leprechaun named Gallaghan, but he is not alone. There is somebody else with him."

"How can you tell?"

"Sometimes I was peeking through the blankets, and I saw that your two rocking chairs in the room were rocking at the same time. Then one of them was rocking while the handle of the wardrobe was moving and making noise. Then the other chair started to rock, and the handle of the door to the hall was turning and making a lot of noise. Sometimes I heard footsteps. I was so scared I hid under the blankets. The noises would stop, and just as I was falling asleep, they would start all over again. They kept me awake until about five o'clock this morning. That is why I got up so late."

"Did you by any chance say to Gallaghan last night that if he was real and living with us you wanted him to come and see you?"

"Yes," she admitted, a little shyly because she had doubted me. "Now I really believe that Little People from other dimensions can come and live with us or just visit us sometimes. What is the name of the other one?"

"I don't know," I said. "The second Little One is new here. When I see Johnny, I will ask him the name of the new one."

Chapter 9

MILADY IS HER NAME

A couple of days after Cathy left, Johnny came to visit us. As we were drinking herb tea, I asked him if he would inquire about the other Little One in the house.

"Of course," he said. "As soon as I know, I will let you know. It won't take long for me to find out."

"Thank you. Take as long as you need," I said. "I'm not in a hurry."

Two days later, Johnny came to my house to tell me about the second visitor. He was laughing.

"I don't have time to stay, but the other Little One is Gallaghan's wife. She came about a week ago to stay with him in your house. I saw her just for a few seconds because she is very, very shy. When she saw me, she hid, and Gallaghan followed her. So I did not have time to ask her name. Sorry. I will try another time."

"Don't be sorry," I said. "You did find out who it was. That's the most important thing for me. In the meantime, I'll name her Milady. Does that sound good to you?"

"Yes. That's a very good name for her. Anyway, if she doesn't like us to call her by that name, she will tell us her true name or Gallaghan will."

As Johnny was leaving, he said, "Have a good time with your Little People, and do not forget that they love you both, you and your mother, and they will protect you and your house."

"Thank you," I said.

We never did find out the real name of Gallaghan's wife. For us, it meant that she liked the name I gave her.

Chapter 10

GALLAGHAN VISITS MY FRIENDS

Gallaghan likes to visit the people I like. Apparently, the Little People can go anywhere they wish at the speed of light and maybe faster.

Let me introduce you to my friend Caroline.

On a late afternoon, while I was relaxing on my couch with a book and a cup of tea, my friend Caroline called me. She was very excited. One of her friends had just left her house, but she took the time to ask me, "How are you?"

"Fine."

"What are you doing? Am I disturbing you?"

"No."

Then she started telling me what had happened in her house that afternoon while she was drinking coffee with one of her friends. About five feet from her, in the window behind her back, a few of her small, white crystals had started to move about and make noise.

Her friend, who was facing that window, asked, "What is happening?"

"Nothing," Caroline had said.

Then, after a little while, the crystals started moving again, but at that time, everything in her window shelf was moving, even the big and small crystals.

Her friend asked again, "What is that? Don't tell me it is nothing. I don't believe you. The window is closed, so I know it isn't the wind."

"You would not understand. You would be scared," she replied.

Caroline knew by then that Gallaghan was visiting her. He likes to visit all my friends.

After her friend had gone, she called me.

"By the way," she told me, "it is not the first time he has visited me, and I really enjoy it. He is always welcome."

Then she asked, "Would it be possible for me to invite the Little People to live in my house?"

"Yes," I said. "You can tell them that they are very welcome. I think they would like to live with you, especially since you have kids and a dog."

Then one day she told me that one of the Little People was staying in her house.

"How did you find out?" I asked.

"Well, he likes to play with the crystals and with our dog. I don't see him, but whenever he is here, the dog runs around the house as though he is chasing someone. And when the dog sits, his head tilts as his eyes watch what I can't see. He never did that before."

Anita, another friend of mine, also received a visit from Gallaghan.

One Thursday afternoon around three o'clock, I answered the phone and heard Anita on the line. She is a little like Johnny in certain ways. She can see and talk with the Little People.

"As I was cleaning my house today," she began, "I heard a small noise behind my back. When I turned around, there was Gallaghan in the living room. He was facing me with a big smile and standing very straight. He was about three feet tall and all dressed up in very colorful clothing. He wore a funny red hat with a green pom-pom, a wide brown belt, green pants, striped green-and-red stockings, soft brown leather boots with pointed toes, and he was holding a smoking pipe in his hands."

I asked him, "What are you doing here? You should not be here. You are supposed to stay at my friend's house and protect her! Gallaghan did listen to me because by the time I finished speaking, he disappeared from my view."

I told Anita that he had not left us alone. "I hope you haven't forgotten that his wife, Milady, is staying with us."

"I was so surprised to see Gallaghan in my living room," Anita said, "that I forgot his wife was also living with you."

Chapter 11

WATCH OUT, NONBELIEVERS!

Two weeks after I spoke to Anita about Gallaghan, I was giving one of my weekend courses in self-healing. I always vacuum the room where the teaching will take place because everybody is going to be sitting on a cushion on the floor.

After lunch, the first day of that weekend, while my students were relaxing outside by the brook, I went into the course room to check if everything was in order. On a small table lay two wooden matches. When the people came back in the room, I asked them, "Who put the matches there?"

One of the attendees named Gilles said, "It was me."

"Is there a reason why you put the matches on the table?"

"No," he said. "I found them on the floor."

"In this room?" I asked.

"Yes," he said, "between you and me . . . where you are sitting."

"They were not there when I was sitting there," I said. I was sure of that.

"Yes, they were not there this morning, but a couple of minutes after you left to go into the kitchen, they were there." Then he added, "Could it be Gallaghan's doing?"

"Yes," I said. Gilles knew about the Little People who were living with us.

"How could this happen?" someone asked.

"Who is Gallaghan?" another person queried.

"Well, well," I said, "my Little People put them there."

"What Little People?" several people asked in unison.

I told them about Gallaghan and Milady and then added, "About two months ago, I spilled nearly a whole box of wooden matches in the other corner of this room. I am pretty sure that Milady and Gallaghan, the leprechauns who live here, took a few."

"Ah," said someone.

"Oh," said another.

"It cannot be possible. You are joking," said one man.

"It's true," said a woman who knew me.

"We have to get back to the course," I laughed. "Our time is limited, but I warn you: Do not ask the leprechauns to prove to you that they are real, especially if you are going to sleep here tonight. If you do, you will get a big surprise during the night."

Four people stayed to sleep over at my house that night. The next morning, we were curious to see how the students had slept. When they came down, they were yawning, their eyes were red, and they were tired because they hadn't slept.

They asked the famous question, "Are they living here?"

Then they said, "We did not believe you. We thought it was impossible that people from another dimension could exist, but *now we believe.*"

Every time I give a course in my home, or in somebody else's home, the subject of the Little People is always raised. Many students do not believe it is true, but let me tell you that they do find out in many different ways, especially those students who stay the night.

The students who sleep in their own houses seldom experience anything on such nights, but not long after they will hear and experience something strange. Then they phone me to ask if either Milady or Gallaghan had visited them.

"Yes, it is possible," I typically say.

But for the ones who sleep in my house, it is another story. They usually get up early, and they try to tell me what happened during the night. They are tired and excited at the same time. Only a few are able to sleep. They are the ones who *believe.*

Only a few people believe, and for Milady and Gallaghan, the unbelievers create an occasion to have lots of fun. They really enjoy the unbelievers. The teasing leprechauns play drums, walk very loudly, and look at people when they turn their backs, so they have to twist around to see who is looking at them. Guests hear somebody either going up or down the stairs; they hear music, and all kinds of noise. The funniest part is that the people who believe in them are not disturbed. The reason why they can sleep so well is that Milady and Gallaghan, like all other Little People from another dimension, can choose by magical ways who is going to hear them, see them, and sometimes feel them.

Chapter 12

A GLIMPSE AT MILADY'S SHOE

A couple of months after giving my weekend course, I was sitting in the kitchen after supper. Around seven o'clock in the evening, while my mother and I were watching television, something on the floor attracted my attention. It was very bright, and it was moving.

"Do you see what I see?" I asked my mother.

"No. What is it?"

"A silvery lady's shoe, shining brightly. It took three steps in front of us. Didn't you see it?"

"No, I didn't."

"The little shoe was about five inches long with a very thin high heel," I said.

The shoe reminded me of pictures of Cinderella's shoe. Prince Charming had tried it on each girl trying to find the right fit.

"Milady was showing me what kind of shoes she was wearing," I said. "They were beautiful. I wish I had a pair exactly like hers."

Milady allowed me to see one of the shoes she was wearing, and what a privilege. Seeing something from another dimension takes a lot of energy from these people.

Chapter 13

THE LITTLE PEOPLE
CAN HELP YOU SOMETIMES

One night, around seven o'clock, a car mechanic came to my house to repair my car. It was a freezing winter night. The mechanic determined that the battery was dead, and he went to a car outlet to get another battery.

In the meantime, I went inside the house and took off my boots, coat, hood, and mittens. When he returned, I had to redress myself in all those very warm clothes to go out and help him. I held a flashlight because he could not see underneath the hood. It was so cold that my hands were numb; my arms felt like ice picks, my teeth were chattering, my whole body was shaking, and the darkness was so deep. If I had not had a flashlight, I would have needed a cane to walk.

After he finished his work, I went inside the house, took off my outdoor clothes, and put them neatly away in the wardrobe. After a few minutes, I went to take a shower. While washing my ears, I noticed one of my earrings was missing.

I looked in the bathtub—nothing. I put my finger in the drain—nothing. After drying myself and putting on my night robe, I went looking all over the house. I checked everywhere I walked after supper because I was wearing both of my earrings at dinnertime.

I said to myself, "Tomorrow morning I will look outside. Maybe I lost it near the car or the porch."

The next morning after breakfast, I dressed myself in my warm winter clothes. It was still very, very cold outside. Some windows in the house were frosted with ice. When I was outside, I looked and looked everywhere we had been the night before: the porch stairs, around the car, and even farther out. No earring. I went inside the house, took all my outside clothes off, shook them, and searched them—nothing. My earring was nowhere to be found.

The earrings were a gift, and I liked them very much. I decided to ask Milady and Gallaghan to find my missing earring and bring it to a place where I could easily find it.

"Please," I begged. "Do it for me; please find my earring. Thank you."

I knew they were listening. Three days later, in the morning, when I returned from the bathroom, I started to make my bed. To make the bed look nice, I have to walk around it a couple of times. When the bed was made, I walked around it again to pick up some clothes from the wardrobe. Between the foot of the bed and the dresser, a few feet from the wardrobe, I stepped on something.

"Ouch!" I cried out. Looking down, do you know what was there? Yes, you do. Of course, you do. It was the missing earring.

I bent down to pick it up and immediately put both of them in my earlobes. I was so happy I could have kissed the leprechauns, so I blew a kiss to Milady and Gallaghan and said, "Thank you. Thank you very much. You are so good to me."

I knew they were there at that moment watching my reactions. You see, it was not the first time I found things that were lost and they were not where I thought I had lost them.

Chapter 14

A DIFFERENT KIND OF HELP

The Little People don't always help you the way you wish.

My aunt Anna came to our house for a vacation. Milady and Gallaghan loved her. They followed Aunt Anna everywhere in the house. Many times during the day, she sensed them very close to her.

One afternoon my mother, her sister Anna, and I were sitting around the kitchen table talking. After a while, my aunt said to me, "You have a beautiful ring."

The ring had an emerald stone set with little diamonds all around it. It was a Christmas gift from Aunt Anna and my mother.

"Did you forget that you and your sister gave it to me two years ago?" I asked my aunt.

"Yes," she said.

I took off the ring intending to hand it to her. She admired it so much that I wanted to give it to her as a gift. As I was dropping the ring in her palm, it was suddenly blown to the floor.

We looked at each other.

"Impossible!" she said. "How could it happen? Our hands were almost touching."

We started to look for the ring. No ring. We took a broom and carefully swept the floor. Still no ring. I ran the vacuum all over the kitchen floor, and then we emptied the vacuum bag on a paper to check for the ring. It was not there.

"I think Milady or Gallaghan want me to keep the ring," I told Aunt Anna.

Three or four days passed after Aunt Anna returned to her house, and we had not yet found the ring.

About one week later, walking back from the front of the house to the kitchen sunroom door, something on the floor near the stairs shone brilliantly. "What's that?" I said to myself.

I bent down to pick it up. Surprise, surprise! It was my emerald ring.

I said aloud to Milady and Gallaghan, "Whoever brought the ring back, I thank you."

Now my mother is wearing the ring. When I gave the ring to her, nothing happened. I guess Milady or Gallaghan wanted my mother to have it. What about Aunt Anna? What does she think about what happened that day?

Amazed is too small a word for it. I do not know why they did that. They simply didn't want my aunt to have the ring.

Chapter 15

SUCH A NICE TOBACCO SMELL!

The tobacco smell can also be an indicator of their presence among us.

Around six o'clock one evening, my mother was washing the dishes. I was sitting about ten feet from her and listening to the news on the television. Suddenly, I started to smell tobacco. The scent was something out of this world. I realized it was pipe tobacco. I took a deep breath, and the scent disappeared. No matter how hard I tried, I could not rekindle the aroma. It was only when I breathed normally that the scent returned.

I asked my mother, who by then was sitting near me, if she smelled it too.

"I don't smell anything," she answered.

"Too bad," I said. "Gallaghan just left. Do you remember the smell of your father's pipe?"

"Yes."

"I also remember it, but I never smelled in all my life such a wonderful aroma as this. It's a much better brand than your father used. Believe me, the aroma of that tobacco is incredible!"

Since that evening, I've never smelled tobacco in my house again. I think Gallaghan must have been watching television with us, and he probably saw all the advertising warnings against tobacco. Since he is very intelligent, he must have stopped smoking when he heard how tobacco can affect your life and make your body sick, especially your lungs.

Chapter 16

MILADY WEARS MY PERFUME

As I said earlier, Milady and Gallaghan liked my aunt Anna very much. Often, Milady would visit my aunt in her house. Aunt Anna knew it was Milady visiting her because when she visited my friends and relatives, she left behind a strong scent of my cologne in the air. Milady would go into houses when nobody was there, and everyone knew she had been there because of the lingering perfume in the air.

The first time Aunt Anna noticed the scent, she had just come into the building. Taking the elevator, she smelled my perfume. She said to herself, "The janitor must have opened the door to let my niece in."

Opening the door to her apartment, the perfume aroma became stronger. Looking around, she called my name, but I was not there.

She phoned to ask me, "Were you in my house today?"

"Of course not," I said. "I am very busy. Having a business at home does not mean I can leave anytime I want. We live sixty miles away from you, remember?"

"Yes," she said, and she told me what had happened to her.

"Well," I said, "every time you smell my cologne, say to yourself that Milady is visiting because she likes my perfume, and she always wears it when she visits my friends."

"In that case," said Aunt Anna, "Milady can come and visit me as often as she wants!"

Milady went often to pay a visit to my aunt Anna, but late one night my aunt had another surprise visit.

It was around one o'clock in the morning, and Aunt Anna could not sleep, so she decided to read in bed. The house was very quiet, and then suddenly, on her lips, she felt a big wet kiss and heard quick little steps going away from her bed toward the entrance of the dining room.

She was so surprised that she dropped the book. It took her a few minutes to realize what had happened and who had done it.

As she was wiping her mouth, she said to herself, laughing, "Only Gallaghan can do such a thing to me. Wait until my niece hears about this."

Early the next morning, her first words to me were, "Guess what that little rascal of yours did to me last night?" She was still laughing and so happy that they liked her so much.

Chapter 17

WONDERFUL GIFTS!

The Little People like Milady and Gallaghan are very nice to have around and living in your house. They protect you. Yes, it's true that sometimes they will take something from you, usually little things, but they will bring them back after a while. Other times, they will only misplace certain objects from one room to another room just to let you know they are still around.

Sometimes they give you a gift. It happened to me one day in a very strange and mysterious way.

As I was dusting the top of my bedroom dresser, I found a very unusual hairpin. It was deep black in color, and its form and material were very different from what I had ever seen before. It was strong, and the indentations were not as marked as other hairpins. The metal was also very unfamiliar to me. I showed it to people from different parts of the world, especially women. Nobody had ever seen a hairpin like it, but I knew where it had come from when I found it on my dresser. It is why I said, "Thank you, Milady, for your gift."

A few weeks after receiving Milady's gift, we were expecting some relatives for the weekend. We had not had guests in our house for a couple of months, so I went to the guest room to vacuum the rug, dust the night table, and check to see if everything was in order, and then I said to myself, "I must wipe the shelves in the wardrobe.

They need it. It is not very nice if you put some clothes on the shelves, and they are full of dust when you take them out."

I dusted the top shelf and found, in the corner of the second shelf, something very odd. I kept looking at it. It had the shape of a small animal bone and almost the same pale color. With two fingers, I picked it up. It was not a bone. It was lightweight and felt like wood. In fact, it was wood!

I knew where it came from because nobody had been in that room for a long time. You would never guess what that little piece of wood looked like. It was about three inches long and very delicate. It was not carved by human hands, but eroded by time and water. This piece of driftwood had the shape of a small beautiful dragon. What a nice gift Gallaghan left me!

One day, as I was shopping in Montreal, I saw a small citrine crystal made like a castle and displayed on a glass table. I couldn't resist buying it. When I returned home, I placed the black hairpin and the little dragon in the citrine castle. They fit perfectly. I put them on the dresser in my bedroom.

Again, I thank Milady and Gallaghan for their beautiful gifts because it is very hard to materialize something from another dimension.

Chapter 18

GALLAGHAN AND MILADY HAVE A NEW COMPANION

I suppose the leprechauns were lonely for the company of another person of their own kind. Playing with dogs and cats was not the same as having another person from their own world. They finally got somebody to join them. How do I know? One night this little fellow came into my dream to see if I would accept him in my house.

Here's the way I learned about the new leprechaun.

In my dream, I was going somewhere with my mother, but I had to go back to the house because I had forgotten something. Stepping into the kitchen, I saw a little fellow coming out of the pantry near the stove. He was coming right through the wood. He was dressed differently than Gallaghan was and appeared to be much younger. I thought maybe he was one of Gallaghan's sons. His sweater was striped green and yellow. On his head he wore a flat hat, a little bigger than a beret. On top of this hat was a pom-pom. He looked to be a very lively and merry little fellow. One of his legs was still inside the pantry, and the other one was in front of him, ready to step onto the kitchen floor.

When he saw me, he stopped. I said, "You can come and live in this house with us. You are very welcome to stay as long as you'd like."

Still in the dream, I returned to my car. As I was driving away from the house, I looked back at one of the kitchen windows. He was standing there waving good-bye with his hand and blowing a kiss toward my mother and me. I forgot to ask his name, so I named him Woody because he came out through a piece of wood. Now Milady and Gallaghan have a little friend with them called Woody.

The next morning, I told my mother about that dream. She was thrilled to learn that another Little One was going to live with us.

Chapter 19

WHY ARE THEY UPSET?

One time Milady and Gallaghan got upset at me. Why were they upset?

Well, my dog, Sam, was very sick. He had an incurable disease. He had two operations in fifteen days, and they were not successful. Sam was old and very weak. One day I took Sam to the veterinarian who kept him until he passed away. Sam moved on to where all animals go when their time comes.

Why didn't I keep Sam a few more days? Sam was too heavy. He weighed one hundred twenty pounds. I could not lift him from the floor and take good care of him. In addition, my house was for sale, and we were moving two hundred miles away. Losing Sam was hard for the leprechauns because they used to play with him. They were losing their home and a friend at the same time. They were very unhappy.

Milady and Gallaghan started to make all kinds of noises to disturb me. They were displacing things, many of the things I needed every day, and I found it annoying.

I asked my friend Johnny, "What's the matter with them? They never behaved like this before. All I can think of is that they think they cannot come with us. They are welcome. You can tell them."

"Tonight I will go to their dimension," Johnny said. "I'll try to talk with them. Tomorrow morning, I'll tell you why they are being so mischievous."

The next afternoon, Johnny phoned. "I had a hard time getting in your house to talk with them. Milady was hiding, and Gallaghan told me that I had no business there. They didn't want to talk to me."

"The lady asked me to come and ask you why you are mad at her," Johnny had told Gallaghan.

At this request, Gallaghan invited Johnny inside the house. He asked Milady to come and join them. They complained to Johnny. "The lady took away Sam, and she is going far away from here."

Johnny explained to them why the dog was no longer at the house, and he told them that they could follow. The new house would be even better than this one. It would be a real country house eight miles from the nearest village. There would be more space, many trees, beautiful wildflowers, and various wild and domestic animals. With smiles on their faces, Milady and Gallaghan told Johnny that they were happier now.

That same night everything was back to normal, and I slept well.

After moving to the country, the Little People were very happy and made themselves at home. Sometimes they would touch Mother very gently on her shoulder just to let us know they were still with us. Milady, Woody, and Gallaghan are my very special little friends.

Chapter 20

GREAT PROTECTORS

Let me tell you how Milady and Gallaghan protect my mother and me within our home.

Sometimes at night, while I am falling asleep, I hear a doorknob rattle. Sometimes I would listen, and then it would stop. I would try to go back to sleep, and as I would begin to get drowsy, the doorknob would start to make noises again. By then, I would know which door was rattling, so I would get up, go downstairs, and check if somebody was trying to get in the house. There was never anybody trying to get inside; it was to remind me that I had forgotten to lock the door before I went to bed.

It never failed. I would always know which of the three outside doors was unlocked. It was fantastic to know. I used to check the other doors too, but it was always the first one I looked at that would be unlocked. The Little People still do that for me even after moving to new places.

They even protected us when we traveled.

One year, my friend Jacqueline and I took a flight to Costa Rica. Well, Milady, Gallaghan, and Woody came to see us there. How did they do that? We all have to guess. The only thing I know is that they can travel and go wherever they want in the blink of an eye. My friend and I had been in Costa Rica for five days. Late one night, Jacqueline and I were lying in our beds, each in a different room, and I could not fall asleep. Something in the air disturbed me, but I didn't know what it was.

Birds started to sing, and horses whinnied. Mother cows called their young ones, dogs barked, and cats meowed. All the noises came from the animals, and they appeared as if they were uncomfortable and as though they were being disturbed.

At the same time, I heard some people playing Ping-Pong outside. I found that little ball bouncing on the table in the middle of the night irritating. I wanted to sleep. It was two o'clock in the morning. I heard ping, pong, pong for about an hour. I thought, "These people should play during the day, not at two o'clock in the morning." Finally, I decided to check out who was playing so late.

I got out of bed, went to the window, and pulled back the drapes. I looked at the open building with a straw roof where the Ping-Pong tables were, but I didn't see anyone. Yet I still heard ping, pong, ping, pong.

Then I realized who was present. As soon as I thought of Milady, Gallaghan, and Woody, the noise stopped. I felt a change in the air. Everything became very quiet. They wanted me to know they had come to visit, and they wanted to be sure that everything was okay. I think they had a ball that night, making everybody feel uncomfortable.

Another time, while I was on my way to Arizona for health reasons, the Little People again came to protect me.

Driving to Arizona, which was about three thousand miles from Montreal, I found the roads in excellent condition even in winter. Only one morning did a little snow come down, though not enough to make me stop and get a motel room. I saw beautiful country scenery, and from one day to the next, the scenery was grand.

Late one afternoon, I stopped at a motel and went in for supper. Back in my room, I took a shower. Sitting on the bed, I read a book before settling in for the night.

After a few minutes, I started to smell my cologne, but I had not used my cologne. The bottle was at the bottom of my suitcase. The smell grew stronger and stronger.

I said, "Hello, Milady. It is nice of you to come and see me. You can sit on the bed near me if you'd like."

She sat down for a few minutes, and then she left. I knew she had left because I could not smell my cologne anymore.

During that same night, I had a bad dream. Whenever I have a bad dream in a city, it means I should not stay in that place.

When I woke up, I knew why Milady had visited me the night before. It was to let me know that once more the Little People were looking after me.

Thank you, Milady, Gallaghan, and Woody, for the protection you are giving my mother and me. Thank you for choosing us as your extended family. We do hope you will always stay with us wherever we go.

Chapter 21

MY BEAUTIFUL FRIEND BARBARA

Let me tell you about the place I found to rest in Arizona. I was exhausted, and I needed a few months to regain my health. I had asked my little friends, the leprechauns, to take a vacation from me as well. My mother had just passed away, and I was planning to sell my house, which was too big for me now.

I went to a place called Pine Valley, a small community about twelve miles from the famous vortex area called Sedona, one hundred miles from Phoenix and about one hundred fifty miles from the Grand Canyon.

Leaving the highway in the direction toward Phoenix, I was surrounded by red mountains of different shapes; some looked like teapots, others like cathedrals. My eyes were not big enough to absorb everything around me, so I pulled over onto the shoulder of the road to avoid an accident. Finally, when I arrived in Sedona, I rented a motel room and called a friend of my Montreal friend to let him know I was in town. He was expecting my call, and he wanted me to go to his house that afternoon because it was Christmas Eve.

"No, I am too tired," I said. "I will meet you tomorrow instead."

The next day, he asked me to stay at his house in Pine Valley until I could find a room to rent. The area was beautiful. I have never seen such different vegetation, trees, birds, and small animals. Everything was so colorful and different from where I lived.

I had a very nice Christmas Day. Few visitors came to see him, and one of them was a charming woman by the name of Barbara. After she left, he told me that she was fixing her house and would like to rent a bedroom.

"Please phone her for me," I said. "I would like to ask her if she could rent me a room for a few months."

The next day, we went to visit her, and two days later, I was living at her house.

It was a beautiful bedroom in a very large home surrounded by tall red rock formations. A big cottonwood tree grew in the front of the house, and there were juniper trees. The earth, rock, and gravel were of various shades of red from pale orange to a deep burgundy-wine color.

Barbara was a very warm and lovely human being. She had six cats that she loved. These cats had been neglected before they came to her. Every time she saw a lost cat, she took it to her house. She had a heart of gold.

We became good friends. We were closer than many sisters in the same family. There was no doubt in my mind that my guardian angels sent her to me. We developed a friendship that will last all our lives.

One day, I was telling Barbara about Milady, Gallaghan, and Woody. She became fascinated. She asked me if she could go and see them. She explained to me that the way she could do it was by traveling in her mind.

"Yes," I said. "They will be happy to see you. I am sure about that because they may be worried about me, and that I am selling the house, which is much too big for me now."

She went to see them, and here is her story.

Chapter 22

BARBARA'S STORY

Not very long ago, Lucile was sent to me by the grace of love to share my house for a few winter months.

Lucile told me the story of Gallaghan and his lady. I was fascinated by all the happenings. Since I can travel out of my body and go wherever I want, I asked her if I could see what the Little Ones were doing.

"Oh, yes," she replied, and at the same time, she asked me to check out how they felt about her move.

So I went.

For me, traveling out of my body is like going to a movie. Up come the pictures. On this specific occasion, I found a white house with green-colored trim situated on a grassy field. I looked into one of the windows. Yes! There they were, Gallaghan, Milady, and Woody. They were playing a dice game; they even crawled over the oval table to get to the rolled dice to toss it again. They were dressed in funny clothes. Gallaghan had on a moss-green shirt with gold buttons. Around his waist was a belt with a buckle that was too big for him. His pants were a darker green. I noticed that they left their hats on the edge of the table.

Milady was wearing a dress. I don't remember what she looked like because I was watching Woody. I could only see Woody's face because he was sitting on a chair, his chin on the table, observing the game.

Woody saw me first. He did not appear to be scared at all. I asked them if I could come in. I told them that I came to see them by request of Lucile.

They stopped playing and made very sad faces.

I asked, "What is going on?"

Gallaghan answered, "We are very disturbed that Lucile is selling this beautiful old house. We love it here. We love the fields, the woods, and the house. It is our home. We feel Lucile will abandon us, and we have no place to go."

"Well," I said, "I'd better tell Lucile about your feelings."

I said good-bye and told them I would return.

Back at my house, I told Lucile about their fears.

"No problem," said Lucile. "They can come with me wherever I go."

Lucile asked me to tell the Little Ones the good news.

The next day, I decided to visit Lucile's house in Canada again, clairvoyantly.

All three of the leprechauns were sitting on chairs by the table, holding their heads up with their hands on their chins. They looked very, very sad.

I knocked on the window and asked if I could come into the house. They seemed happy to see me. All three of them started to talk at the same time, asking me all kinds of questions. I let them finish first, and then I told them that Lucile would find another beautiful place where all of them, including Lucile, could have a lot of fun.

This appeared to be wonderful music to their ears because they started to dance. Gallaghan even took his hat off and flung it in the air. I said good-bye and left.

The next day, I went to check out how they were doing without letting them know I was there. I saw them having a lot of fun playing dice again, and they were smiling and laughing.

Chapter 23

THE BIGGEST TRICK EVER PLAYED ON ME

After I sold my farm in the country, my youngest son and I bought a house in Mont Saint-Hilaire, a small city near Montreal. The town is full of visitors who come to pick up apples and buy the famous iced apple cider made from the fruit that grows in the area and is ready in the winter.

There was so much traffic around the area that my son felt it was not safe for me to live alone in this big house, so he suggested that I should have an alarm system installed and connected to the police station.

"Then I would not have to worry about you," my son said.

"Well, do what you want. I really don't need it; I am well protected," I answered.

About ten days after the alarm system was installed, while I was talking on the phone with a friend, the front doorbell rang.

"I have to let you go. There is someone at the door. I will call you back," I said to my friend.

I opened the door, and guess who was standing in front of me? A police officer.

"Are you having some trouble, ma'am?" he asked.

"No," I said. "Why are you here?"

"Your alarm rang at the station. Are you sure you are okay?"

"Yes. The alarm is not on. I don't understand," I told him. "Can you please check the alarm?"

"You are right," he said. "It is not on. Your son was worried. He could not reach you because your phone was busy."

"I will phone him to reassure him," I said.

As I was walking toward the telephone, my son called. I told him what had happened.

"I was worried about you, Mom," he said. "Hope you are fine."

"Don't worry about me. I am okay."

After fifteen to twenty minutes later, the doorbell rang again, and I went to answer it.

Well, it was the same police officer, and he did not appear too happy this time.

"You have trouble again, ma'am?" he asked.

"No."

"If it happens again, there will be a charge," he said.

"Yes, sir," I said. "I will ask my son to contact the company and get the system checked."

The next morning, around nine o'clock, a man from the alarm company came to check the whole system. He did not find anything wrong with it. Everything was in order.

This man told me he was the owner of the company, and it was the first time that one of his systems had failed.

"I know what happened," I said. "After the second time the police came to my home."

"You know?" he asked.

I asked him, "Do you believe in Little People from other dimensions visiting us and sometimes living with us?"

"Yes," he said.

I knew he was telling the truth, and he started to ask me all kinds of questions about them.

"I have three different leprechauns living with me," I said. "The oldest one, Gallaghan, plays tricks on me, and that is his way to let me know he is still protecting me, wherever I am. That's what happened last night. So I told Gallaghan to please not do that again because the police department is very upset."

The man could not get over the kinds of tricks these Little People play on humans.

Since talking to Gallaghan, I have not had any more trouble with the alarm system, and I thank him for still taking care of me.

Chapter 24

THEY ARE BACK!

After I left Mont Saint-Hilaire, I lost track of my little friends, the leprechauns, for many years until recently when I decided to finalize this book. They came back in force. One night, while we were editing the book, Gallaghan came to see us, and he played some tricks on the computer keyboard. The cursor was moving all over the place, and we were having difficulty writing. We were laughing. He made us feel very good.

One day, I was feeling very sick, so I asked my spiritual daughter, Jojo, to take me to emergency. The doctors kept me at the hospital for a few days. But when we left for the hospital, we had to leave the doors open because Jojo had just painted them that morning. When she returned home, around ten o'clock that night, everything appeared nice and untouched, but a surprise was waiting for her. She heard the three different doorbells of the house ringing, one after the other for about half an hour. It was driving her crazy. Curious, she tried the doorbell and realized it was not the same sound. She thought that was weird, but finally all the noise stopped, and she went to sleep.

The next day, when she visited me at the hospital, she told me about this event. Right away, I asked her whether the dogs had barked, because they usually do bark a lot when somebody comes to one of the doors. She said she checked every door, but nobody was there.

"No," she said. "They didn't bark."

Then I told her, "My dear Jojo, you just got your first experience with my little friends the leprechauns."

When the Little People come and live with you, you don't know how long they will stay because they have many things to learn from you in this dimension. They will stay as long as they need to stay to know you better, and then they have to go along with their own lives, sometimes with other humans or sometimes back in their dimension.

My stories with Milady, Gallaghan, and Woody will never end. I know they will keep visiting me until the end of my time on earth.

I have more stories to tell you about them, but until that time, I wish for you, readers, that a little leprechaun will come and live with you so your life will be filled with magic and love.

The End